The Spinning Blackboard and Other Dynamic Experiments on Force and Motion

THE EXPLORATORIUM SCIENCE SNACKBOOK SERIES

The Spinning Blackboard and Other Dynamic Experiments on Force and Motion

◀▶

THE EXPLORATORIUM SCIENCE SNACKBOOK SERIES

PAUL DOHERTY, DON RATHJEN
and the Exploratorium Teacher Institute

JOHN WILEY & SONS, INC.
New York · Chichester · Brisbane · Toronto · Singapore

Development and Testing   Teachers of the Exploratorium Teacher Institute
Photography   Esther Kutnick, Susan Schwartzenberg, Amy Snyder
Illustrations   Larry Antila, Jad King, Arthur Koch, Luisa Kolla, Peter Olguin

This text is printed on acid-free paper.

Library of Congress Cataloging-in-Publication Data:

Doherty, Paul.
    The spinning blackboard and other dynamic experiments on force and motion / Paul Doherty, Don Rathjen, and the Exploratorium Teacher Institute.
        p.   cm. — (The Exploratorium science snackbook series)
    Includes index.
    Summary: Presents over twenty experiments exploring the principles of mechanics. The experiments are miniature versions of some of the exhibits at the Exploratorium, San Francisco's famed museum of science, art, and human perception.
    ISBN 0-471-11514-2 (pbk. : alk. paper)
    1. Force and energy—Experiments.   2. Force and energy—Study and teaching (Elementary)   3. Force and energy—Study and teaching (Secondary)   4. Motion—Experiments.   5. Motion—Study and teaching (Elementary)   6. Motion—Study and teaching (Secondary)   7. Science museums—Educational aspects.   [1. Mechanics—Experiments.   2. Experiments.]   I. Rathjen, Don.   II. Exploratorium Teacher Institute (San Francisco, Calif.)   III. Title.   IV. Series.
QC73.D63   1996
531'.112'078—dc20   95-10878

Printed in the United States of America

10 9 8 7 6 5 4 3 2 1

To the many teachers of the Exploratorium Teacher Institute

who enthusiastically developed and tested

the materials in this book.

Contents

Welcome to the Exploratorium Science Snackbook Series

This book is full of Snacks...

...but they're not the kind you eat. They're the kind you can learn from and have fun with.

Exploratorium Science Snacks are miniature versions of some of the most popular exhibits at the Exploratorium, San Francisco's famed museum of science, art, and human perception.

What's different about the Exploratorium?

For lack of a better description, the Exploratorium calls itself a "museum." But the half-million visitors who come through the doors each year don't find hushed corridors, watchful guards, or "do not touch" signs. Instead, they walk into a cavernous space filled with whirring, buzzing, spinning things, where people of all ages are smiling and laughing and calling to each other to "Come see this!" and "Hey, look at that!"

At the Exploratorium, you can touch a tornado, look inside your eye, or leave your shadow on a wall. You can pull a giant bubble over your head, sing your way through a maze, or tour a pitch-dark labyrinth using only your sense of touch. When you're done, you might find that you understand a little more about weather, or your senses, or the nature of a bubble film, than you've ever understood before.

So what's a Science Snack?

Since the museum opened in 1969, teachers from the San Francisco Bay Area have brought their classes on field trips to the Exploratorium. When we began putting this book together, we decided to do just the opposite: We wanted to take the exhibits to the kids.

For three years, nearly one hundred teachers worked with staff members to create scaled-down versions of Exploratorium exhibits. The results were dozens of exciting "Snacks"— miniature science exhibits that teachers could make using common, inexpensive, easily available materials. By using Snacks in their classrooms, teachers can climb out of their textbooks and join their students in discovering science for themselves.

What's in a Snack?

The Snacks in this book are divided into easy-to-follow sections that include instructions, advice, and helpful hints.

Each Snack begins with a drawing of the original, full-sized exhibit on the museum floor and a photograph of the scaled-down version that you can make yourself. A short paragraph introduces the exhibit. There's a list of the materials needed and suggestions on how to find them. Other sections give assembly instructions, contain descriptions of how to use the completed exhibits, and explain the science behind them. Most of the Snacks can be completed by one person. If a partner or adult help is needed, this is indicated. A section called "etc." offers interesting bits of additional scientific and historic information.

What can you do with a Snack?

The original collection of 107 Science Snacks was published in a single volume called *The Exploratorium Science Snackbook*. Although the book was written for local high school science teachers, it wasn't long before we began to realize that Snacks were really getting around. Within a week of publication, for instance, we received a message from a teacher in the Australian outback who needed help finding materials.

We heard from elementary school teachers and university professors. Art teachers were using Snacks, as were shop teachers and math teachers. Sixth-graders at one school were building their own miniature science museum. At another school, an ESL (English as a Second Language) teacher found that building Snacks helped her students interact more: The ones who understood science best were helping those more adept at building things, and all were getting better at communicating with each other.

And it wasn't just teachers who found Snacks useful: Children were bringing Snacks home to their families. Scouts were using Snacks to help get science badges; Snacks were making appearances at science fairs, birthday parties, and impromptu "magic" shows.

Try it for yourself!

Until now, Science Snacks were available only to teachers. The books in this series now make Science Snacks available to anyone interested in learning about science, or helping others learn about science. Try it for yourself! You might be delighted to find how well hands-on discovery works.

Acknowledgments

The production of the original *Exploratorium Science Snackbook*,
upon which this book is based, was made possible
by a grant from

The Telesis Foundation

The Snackbook was developed by the Teacher Institute, a part
of the Exploratorium Regional Science Resource Center, which is
funded in part by

California Department of Education
National Science Foundation
Walter S. Johnson Foundation

What This Book Is About

Chances are you know more about the principles of physics than you suspect. Just to get by in the world, you need to understand something about forces and how they affect motion.

Suppose, for example, you had a choice: You could stand in the path of a charging rhino, or you could stand in the path of a charging mouse. I'm sure you know that it would be harder to stop the rhino than it would be to stop the mouse. That means you have an intuitive understanding of Newton's Second Law of Motion, which says that the force you need to make something slow down (or speed up) depends on how massive that something is. Since the rhino is considerably more massive than the mouse, it takes more force to stop it.

There are many situations in which you rely on your knowledge of physics. Imagine that you had to balance on a narrow board and walk like a tightrope walker over a deep abyss. To help yourself balance, you'd probably stretch your arms out to the sides. You know that extending your arms makes balancing easier, even if you don't know why.

Or suppose the rear wheels of your car are stuck in an icy ditch. If you gun the engine, the wheels spin. Some friends come to help you push the car out, but even when you work together, you can't push the car out all at once. So you start it rocking. You push it forward, let it roll back, then push it forward again, matching the timing of your pushes to the rhythm of the car's movement. With each forward push, the car moves farther—until it finally rolls up out of the ditch. When you rock the car, you are applying a small force repeatedly at just the right time in order to cause a very large motion—a process that physicists call *resonance.*

The experiments in this book are designed to help you examine some of the physical principles that you apply in your everyday life. With the "Momentum Machine," for example, you can go for a spin and learn more about how changing your weight distribution can change your motion. You will also find out why ice skaters and ballet dancers twirl faster when they pull their arms in.

Three experiments involving resonance—"Resonant Pendulum," "Resonant Rings," and "Resonator"—will help you understand how rocking a car helps you get it out of a ditch. Along the way, you'll also learn about one reason an earthquake may knock down certain buildings and leave others standing.

With "Falling Feather," you can prove that Galileo was right: A heavy weight and a light weight accelerate toward the ground at the same rate. If you drop a feather and a penny in a vacuum, they hit the ground at exactly the same time. With "Bicycle Wheel Gyro," you can make a giant gyroscope from a bicycle wheel and experience firsthand the forces that a gyroscope exerts.

Taken together, the experiments in this book will help you understand some basic physical principles and link them to your existing knowledge of the world around you. Have fun!

Balancing Ball

Suspend a ball in a stream of air.

▶ A ball stably levitated on an invisible stream of air is a dramatic sight. When you try to pull the ball out of the airstream, you can feel a force pulling it back in. You can also feel that the airstream is being deflected by the ball. This Snack shows one of the forces that give airplanes lift.

Materials

Small Snack

> ► A hair dryer (blower).
>
> ► A spherical balloon or table tennis ball.
>
> ► Tissue paper.
>
> ► Optional: a stand for the blower.

Large Snack

> ► A vacuum cleaner with a reversible hose so it can be used as blower, such as a Shop Vac™.
>
> ► A light-weight vinyl beach ball.
>
> ► Tissue paper.
>
> ► Optional: A stand for the hose.

Assembly

None required. Note, though, that you can make a large or a small Snack (see "Materials"). Depending on the blower you choose, some experimentation may be necessary to find a satisfactory ball. You might want a partner to help you, or you can devise some sort of stand for the blower. That way, your hands will be free to experiment with the ball in the airstream.

To Do and Notice
(5 minutes or more)

Blow a stream of air straight up. Carefully balance the ball above the airstream. Pull it slowly out of the flow. Notice that when only half the ball is out of the airstream, you can feel it being sucked back in. Let go of the ball and notice that it oscillates back and forth and then settles down near the center of the airstream.

With one hand, pull the ball partially out of the airstream. With the other hand, dangle a piece of tissue paper and search for the airstream above the ball. Notice that the ball deflects the airstream outward. On the large version of this Snack, you can actually feel the deflected airstream hit your hand.

Tilt the airstream to one side and notice that the ball can still be suspended.

Balance the ball in the airstream and then move the blower and the ball toward a wall (try the corner of a room). Notice the great increase in height of the suspended ball.

What's Going On?

When the ball is suspended in the airstream, the air flowing upward hits the bottom of the ball and slows down, generating a region of higher pressure. The high-pressure region of air under the ball holds the ball up against the pull of gravity.

When you pull the ball partially out of the airstream, the air flows around the curve of the ball that is nearest the center of the airstream. Air rushes in an arc around the top of the ball and then continues outward above the ball.

This outward-flowing air exerts an inward force on the ball, just like the downward flow of air beneath a helicopter exerts an upward force on the blades of the helicopter. This explanation is based on Newton's law of action and reaction.

Another way of looking at this is that as the air arcs around the ball, the air pressure on the ball decreases, allowing the normal atmospheric pressure of the calm air on the other side of the ball to push the ball back into the airstream.

People immediately raise several questions when they hear the second explanation:

Why does air flowing over a surface in an arc exert less pressure on that surface? To answer this question, consider a rider in a roller coaster going over the top of a hill at high speed. The force that the rider exerts on the seat decreases as the rider goes over the top of the hill. In the same way, the air that arcs around the side of the ball exerts less force on the ball.

Why does air follow the surface of the sphere? Consider what would happen if the air did not curve around the ball. An "air shadow" would be formed above the ball. This air shadow would be a region of low pressure. The air would then flow into the low-pressure air shadow. So the air flows around the ball.

An alternative explanation is provided by the Bernoulli principle. If you pull the ball far enough out of the airstream, then the air flows over only one side of the ball. In fact, the airstream speeds up as it flows around the ball. This is because the middle of the ball sticks farther into the airstream than the top or bottom. Since the same amount of air must flow past all parts of the ball each second, it must flow faster where it is pinched together at the middle. The Bernoulli principle states that where air speeds up, its pressure drops. The difference in pressure between the still air and the moving air pushes the ball back into the center of the airstream.

When you approach a wall with the balanced ball, the high-pressure region under the ball becomes a region of even higher pressure. The air that hits the bottom of the ball can no longer expand outward in the direction of the wall. The higher pressure drives the ball to a greater height.

○ ○ ○ ○ ○ ○   **etc.**   ○ ○ ○ ○ ○ ○

This exhibit illustrates one of the reasons that airplanes fly. A flat wing will fly if it is tipped into the wind, so that it forces air downward. Newton's third law tells us that for every action there must be an equal and opposite reaction: The reaction to the downward force of the wing on the air is the upward force of the air on the wing. You can feel this lifting force if you hold your hand out the window of a moving car and tip your hand so that it forces the air downward.

A wing that is curved on top will deflect air downward and produce lift even if it isn't tipped. The explanation for this is essentially the same as the one given in this Snack. The wing collides with air, creating a region of high pressure in front of the wing. This high pressure produces *drag,* which is always associated with *lift.* The high-pressure air in front of the wing accelerates air over the curved surface of the wing. This air then flows downward behind the wing. Airplanes fly because their wings throw air downward.

It is sometimes said that air must flow faster over the curved top surface of a wing than over the flat bottom. This is said to happen because the air has to meet up again at the far end of the wing, and since the air traveling over the curved path must travel farther, it must travel faster. This is not true. Two parcels of air that start together, then split to flow over different sides of a wing, do not, as a rule, rejoin at the far end of the wing.

Balancing Stick

Does it matter which end is up?

▶ The distribution of the mass of an object determines the position of its center of gravity, its angular momentum, and your ability to balance it!

Materials ▸ One ½ inch (1.25 cm) wooden dowel, approximately 3 feet (90 cm) long.

▸ A lump of clay.

Assembly
(5 minutes or less)

Place a lump of clay about the size of your fist 8 inches (20 cm) from the end of the dowel.

To Do and Notice
(5 minutes or more)

Balance the stick on the tip of your finger, putting your finger under the end that's near the clay. Now turn the stick over and balance it with the clay on the top. Notice that the stick is easier to balance when the clay is near the top.

What's Going On?

The dowel rotates more slowly when the mass is at the top, allowing you more time to adjust and maintain balance. When the mass is at the bottom, the stick has less *rotational inertia* and tips more quickly. The farther away the mass is located from the axis of rotation (such as in your hand), the greater the rotational inertia and the slower the stick turns. An object with a large mass is said to have a great deal of inertia. Just as it is hard to change the motion of an object that has a large inertia, it is hard to change the rotational motion of an object with a large rotational inertia.

You can feel the change in inertia when you do the following experiment. Grab the end of the dowel that's near the clay. Hold the dowel vertically, and rapidly move the dowel back and forth with the same motion you would use to cast a fishing line. Next, turn the dowel upside down, and hold it at the end that is farthest from the clay. Repeat the casting motion. Notice that it is much harder to move the dowel rapidly when the clay is near the top. The mass of the stick has not changed, but the distribution of the mass of the stick with respect to your hand has changed. The rotational inertia depends on the distribution of the mass of the stick.

○ ○ ○ ○ ○ ○   **etc.**   ○ ○ ○ ○ ○ ○

As an alternative, do not demonstrate the Snack in advance. Instead, give a group of people the clay and dowel separately, and challenge them to see who can balance the dowel the longest. Let them discover the role of the clay.

Bernoulli Levitator

Suspend an object in the air by blowing down on it.

▶ *The Bernoulli principle explains how atomizers work and why windows are sometimes sucked out of their frames as two trains rush past each other. You can choose from two versions of this Snack—small or large.*

Materials

Small Snack

> ▸ A large wood or plastic thread spool.
> ▸ An index card.
> ▸ A pushpin.
> ▸ Optional: Drinking straws.

Large Snack

> ▸ A hair dryer or vacuum-cleaner blower.
> ▸ A stiff paper or plastic plate.
> ▸ A cardboard box with one side somewhat larger than the plate.
> ▸ A pushpin.

Small Snack

Assembly
(5 minutes or less)

Trim an index card to a 3 × 3 inch (7.5 × 7.5 cm) square. Push the pushpin into the card's center.

If more than one person is going to use this, construct the following sanitary version: Cut a 2 inch (5 cm) long piece of straw for each person. At each person's turn, have him or her push one end of the straw into the hole in the spool of thread. If any straw does not fit, cut a ¼ inch (6.25 mm) slit near the end of the straw and push it into the spool.

To Do and Notice
(5 minutes or more)

Hold the card against the bottom of the spool with the pushpin sticking into the spool's hole. The pushpin keeps the card from drifting off to the side.

Blow strongly through the hole in the top of the spool and let go of the card. If the card falls at first, experiment with different-sized cards or spools until you can make the card hang suspended beneath the spool.

Large Snack

Assembly
(15 minutes or less)

Cut the flaps off the top of the box, and turn the box so that the opening faces to the side. Put the side of the box that is larger than the plate on top, and cut a hole in the center slightly smaller than the outlet of the hair dryer or vacuum hose.

Stick a pushpin through the center of the plate.

To Do and Notice
(5 minutes or more)

Turn on the blower and direct it down through the hole. If you use a vacuum cleaner, be sure to use it as a blower. If you use a hair dryer, turn the heat off if you can. (If you can't, the hair dryer may overheat and automatically turn off. It will work again as soon as it cools down.)

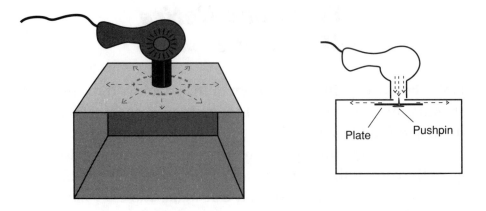

Bring the plate up toward the hole from below. Contrary to what you might expect, as the plate approaches the hole it will be sucked up and held in place by the air blowing down. The pushpin should keep the plate from drifting off to the side.

For Both Snacks

What's Going On?

When you blow into the spool or through the box, the air goes through the opening, hits the card or plate, and accelerates outward. The energy needed to accelerate the air comes from the energy stored as compression of the gas, so the gas expands, and its pressure drops.

As air (or any other fluid) accelerates, its pressure drops. This is known as the *Bernoulli principle*. In the small version of this Snack, the air rushing between the spool and the card exerts less pressure on the card than the still air underneath the card. The still air pushes the card toward the spool and holds the card up against gravity. In the larger version, the same principle is at work, holding the plate up against the hole in the box.

○ ○ ○ ○ ○ ○ **etc.** ○ ○ ○ ○ ○ ○

In an atomizer, or perfume sprayer, you squeeze a rubber bulb to squirt air through a tube. Because of the Bernoulli principle, the air rushing through the tube has a lower pressure than the surrounding atmosphere. Atmospheric pressure forces the perfume up an intersecting tube into the low-pressure airstream. The perfume is pushed out of the tube and sprays into the air as a fine mist.

The air rushing through the space between two moving trains also has a lower pressure, due to the Bernoulli principle. Sometimes, the higher pressure, stationary air inside each train forces some of the trains' windows out of their frames.

Bicycle Wheel Gyro

A bicycle wheel acts like a giant gyroscope.

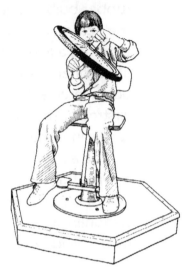

▶ In the weightless environment of the space shuttle, the astronauts experimented with a toy gyroscope. Even when an astronaut gave the spinning gyro a shove, the toy's axle stubbornly resisted changing direction. Any rapidly spinning wheel exhibits this gyroscopic property. A spinning bicycle wheel resists efforts to tilt it and point the axle in a new direction. You can use this tendency to take yourself for an unexpected spin.

Materials ▶ A bicycle wheel. (Cheap or free from a thrift shop, a bike store, or your friends.)

▶ 2 handles. (Plastic handles from a hardware store work perfectly and are cheap. Get the kind of handle that is designed to screw onto a file.)

▶ A low friction rotating stool or platform. (Typing or computer chairs often work well.)

▶ Optional: Eyebolt; drill; chain or rope suspended from a large stand or a ceiling; spoke guards.

▶ Adult help.

Assembly
(15 minutes or less)

Screw the handles onto each side of the wheel's axle. You may have to remove the outer nuts to clear enough axle for the hand-

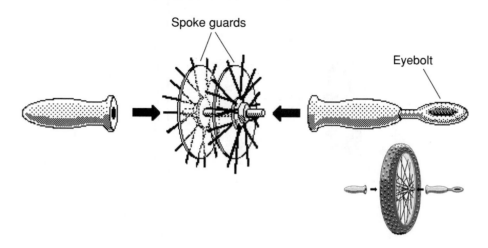

Spoke guards

Eyebolt

les. You may want to put plastic spoke guards on the hubs first to protect your fingers from the spinning wheel.

If you have the eyebolt, drill a hole in the end of one handle for it. Mount the screw eye in the hole.

To Do and Notice
(15 minutes or more)

Hold the wheel by the handles while another person gets it spinning as fast as possible. Sit on the stool with your feet off the floor, and tilt the wheel. If the stool has sufficiently low friction, the stool should start to turn. Tilt the wheel in the other direction.

Get the wheel spinning, and then use the eyebolt in the end of the handle to hang the wheel from a hook mounted to the free end of a chain or rope. Hold the wheel so that the axle is horizontal, then release it. The axle will remain more or less horizontal while it moves slowly in a circle.

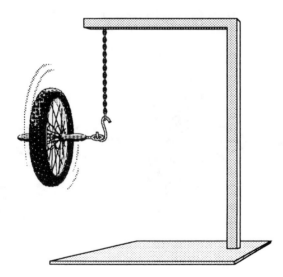

If you don't have a chain or rope, rest the eyebolt on your fingertips. Be sure to practice this before you try a demonstration. You will have to move with the wheel as it slowly turns in a circle.

What's Going On?

A rotating bicycle wheel has *angular momentum*, which is a property involving the speed of rotation, the mass of the wheel, and how the mass is distributed. For example, most of a bicycle wheel's mass is concentrated along the wheel's rim, rather than at the center, and this causes a larger angular momentum at a given speed. Angular momentum is characterized by both size and direction.

The bicycle wheel, you, and the chair comprise a system that obeys the principle of *conservation of angular momentum*. This means that any change in angular momentum within the system must be accompanied by an equal and opposite change, so the net effect is zero.

Suppose you are now sitting on the stool with the bicycle wheel spinning. One way to change the angular momentum of the bicycle wheel is to change its direction. To do this, you must exert a twisting force, called a *torque*, on the wheel. The bicycle wheel will then exert an equal and opposite torque on you. (That's because for every action there is an equal and opposite reaction.) Thus, when you twist the bicycle wheel in space, the bicycle wheel will twist you the opposite way. If you are sitting on a low-friction pivot, the twisting force of the bicycle wheel will cause you to turn. The change in angular momentum of the wheel is compensated for by your own change in angular momentum. The system as a whole ends up obeying the principle of conservation of angular momentum.

Unfortunately, the gyroscopic precession of the wheel hanging from the rope is not explainable in as straightforward a manner as the rotating stool effect. However, the effect itself is well worth experiencing, even though its explanation is too difficult to undertake here. For more information, consult any college physics text under *precession*.

Bubble Suspension

Soap bubbles float on a cushion of carbon dioxide gas.

▶ This beautiful experiment illustrates the principles of buoyancy, semipermeability, and interference.

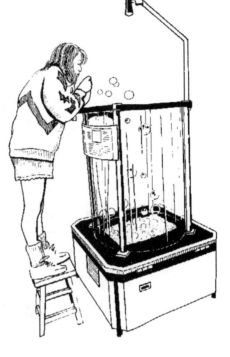

Materials   ▸ A small aquarium.

▸ Dry ice.

▸ Bubble solution. You can use a commercial solution like Wonder Bubbles™, or use the Exploratorium's recipe: ⅔ cup (160 ml) Dawn™ dishwashing liquid and 1 tablespoon (15 ml) glycerine (available at most drugstores) in 1 gallon (3.8 l) of water. Aging the solution for at least a day before use significantly increases the lifetime of the bubbles.

▸ Gloves.

▸ Adult help.

Assembly
(5 minutes or less)

Place a slab of dry ice flat in the bottom of the aquarium. (CAUTION: Use gloves when handling the dry ice; do not touch it with bare skin.) Allow a few minutes for a layer of carbon dioxide gas to accumulate.

To Do and Notice
(15 minutes or more)

Blow bubbles so they float down into the aquarium. The bubbles will descend and then hover on the denser layer of carbon dioxide gas. After a few minutes, notice that the bubbles begin to expand and sink. Notice the color bands on the bubbles. Notice how some of the bubbles freeze on the dry ice.

What's Going On?

As dry ice turns from a solid to a vapor, or *sublimes*, it produces carbon dioxide gas. Carbon dioxide is denser than air. (Carbon dioxide molecules have an atomic mass of 44 amu [atomic mass units]. Air is made up of nitrogen, 28 amu, and oxygen, 32 amu.) The denser carbon dioxide gas forms a layer on the bottom of the aquarium.

A bubble is full of air. It floats on the carbon dioxide layer just like a helium balloon floating in the air. You might expect that the air in the bubble would cool and contract near the dry ice, but the bubble actually expands slightly. The soapy wall of the bubble allows carbon dioxide to pass through but does not allow air molecules to pass through. Initially, the concentration of carbon dioxide gas is low inside the bubble and high outside the bubble. The gas gradually diffuses into the bubble, a process called *osmosis*. The bubble film is a *semipermeable membrane*— a surface that allows some substances to pass through while

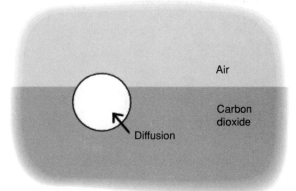

preventing others from passing through at all. The cells in your body have the same property. Water, oxygen, and carbon dioxide easily enter some cells, whereas other molecules do not. The added carbon dioxide makes the bubble denser, causing it to gradually sink. The carbon dioxide at the bottom of the tank is cold enough to freeze the bubble.

○ ○ ○ ○ ○ ○   **etc.**   ○ ○ ○ ○ ○ ○

You can do many experiments with these bubbles.

What happens when bubbles of different sizes collide? Sometimes they make a single larger bubble, other times they join as two bubbles with a flat or bulging wall between them. If the two bubbles are the same size, the wall is flat between them, since the pressure is equal on both sides. If the two bubbles are of different sizes, the wall will bulge away from the smaller of two bubbles, since the smaller bubble will have a higher pressure inside.

How does a bubble respond to a comb that has been charged by rubbing it with a wool cloth? The neutral bubble is electrically polarized by, and attracted to, the charged comb.

Bubble Tray

Create giant bubbles.

▶ Bubbles are fascinating. What gives them their shape? What makes them break or last? What causes the colors and patterns in the soap film, and why do they change?

Materials ► Measuring cups and spoons.

► Dawn™ or other dishwashing liquid.

► Glycerine (available at drugstores).

► Tap water.

► A wire coat hanger.

► A shallow tub or tray about 18 inches (45 cm) in diameter (such as a potted-plant drain dish, a pizza pan, or a catering tray).

► Optional: Yarn.

Assembly
(30 minutes or less)

Mix up a bubble solution of ⅔ cup (160 ml) Dawn™ dishwashing liquid and 1 tablespoon (15 ml) glycerine in one gallon (3.8 l) of water. We have found that more durable bubbles form if you let this solution age for at least a day, preferably for a week.

Bend the coat hanger into a flat hoop with the hook sticking up at an angle to serve as a handle. Bubbles will form more consistently when the hoop is as circular as possible. If you wrap yarn tightly around the wire of the hoop, the yarn will absorb the bubble solution, which will make the hoop easier to use.

If you prefer a more elegant apparatus, a bubble tray complete with a bubble hoop is available at the Exploratorium Store for about $20.

To Do and Notice
(15 minutes or more)

Fill the shallow tray with bubble solution and submerge the hoop in the solution. Then tilt the hoop toward you until it is almost vertical, and lift it from the tray. You should have a bubble film extending across the hoop. Swing the hoop through the air to make a giant bubble. When you have a big bubble, twist the hoop to seal it off at the end.

What shapes do the bubbles take once they are free of the hoop? What roles do convection and air currents play in the bubble's movement? Look for patterns and colors in the bubbles. Dip the hoop in the solution and hold it up to the light without forming a bubble. What patterns (and changes in patterns) do you observe?

What's Going On?

The strong mutual attraction of water molecules for each other is known as *surface tension.* Normally, surface tension makes it impossible to stretch the water out to make a thin film. Soap reduces the surface tension and allows a film to form.

Because of surface tension, a soap film always pulls in as tightly as it can, just like a stretched balloon. A soap film makes the smallest possible surface area for the volume it contains. If the bubble is floating in the air and makes no contact with other objects, it will form a sphere, because a sphere is the shape that has the smallest surface area compared to its volume. (Wind or vibration may distort the sphere.)

The patterns of different colors in a soap bubble are caused by *interference.* Light waves reflected from the inner and outer surfaces of the soap film interfere with each other *constructively* or *destructively*, depending on the thickness of the bubble and the wavelength (that is, the color) of the light. For example, if the soap film is thick enough to cause waves of red light to interfere destructively with each other, the red light is eliminated, leaving only blue and green to reach your eyes.

○ ○ ○ ○ ○ ○   **etc.**   ○ ○ ○ ○ ○ ○

You can make other devices to create large bubbles.
One of the easiest is a length of string (or, still better,
fuzzy yarn) threaded through two drinking straws,
with the ends tied to make a loop any size you want.
Not only will this device make large bubbles, but you
can twist the straws to make film surfaces with
different shapes.

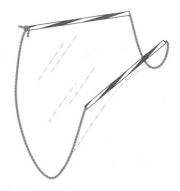

Center of Gravity

How to balance a checkbook using the physics method.

► *Here is an easy way to find the center of gravity of a long, thin object, even if the object's weight is unevenly distributed.*

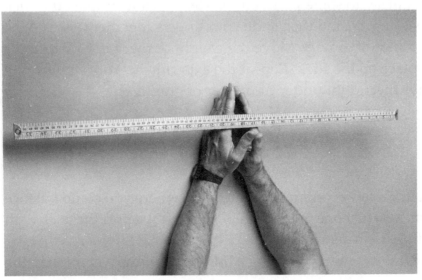

Materials ▸ A meterstick, cane, or any stick of similar
                length.
             ▸ Clay or weight.
             ▸ Masking tape.

Assembly
(5 minutes or less)

First try the experiment with just the stick itself. Then tape the
clay or weight somewhere on the stick and try again.

To Do and Notice
(5 minutes or more)

Support the stick by resting each of its ends on a finger. Slowly
slide your fingers together until they meet. Your fingers will
meet under the stick's *center of gravity*. Attach the weight or a
piece of clay to some point on the stick. Again support the stick
on two fingers, and then slide your fingers together to locate the
new center of gravity. Move the weight or piece of clay to some
new place on the stick. Repeat the experiment. Your fingers will
always meet right under the center of gravity.

What's Going On?

The stick's center of gravity is the place where you could balance
the stick on just one finger. When you first support the stick with
two fingers, in general one finger (the one that is closer to the center of gravity) will be holding a little more of the weight than the

other. When you try to move your fingers closer together, the one that is carrying less weight will slide more easily. This finger will continue to slide more easily until it gets closer to the center of gravity than the other finger, at which point the situation will reverse and the other finger will begin to slide faster. Your left and right fingers simply alternate moving until they meet at the center of gravity, where both fingers support equal weight.

Coupled Resonant Pendulums

These pendulums trade swings back and forth.

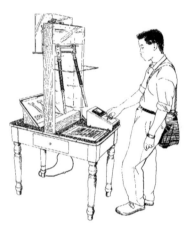

▶ Two pendulums suspended from a common support will swing back and forth in intriguing patterns if the support allows the motion of one pendulum to influence the motion of the other.

Materials ▶ 2 plastic 35 mm film cans.

▶ Clay, coins, or washers for mass.

▶ 2 pieces of metal coat hanger wire, each about 8 inches (20 cm) long.

▶ A piece of string about 3 feet (90 cm) long.

▶ 2 ring stands or other vertical supports for the string.

Assembly
(30 minutes or less)

Stretch and secure the string between two ring stands placed about 20 to 30 inches (50 to 75 cm) apart. In the center of each film can lid, punch a hole just large enough to insert one end of a coat hanger wire. Bend the end of the inserted wire so the lid won't slide off but so that you can still put the lid on the can. Bend the other end of the wire so it will hang freely from the string. The two hangers should be close to the same length. Add equal amounts of clay, coins, or washers to each can and attach the lids. Hang the pendulums so that they are about equally spaced from each other and from the ring stands.

To Do and Notice
(15 minutes or more)

Gently pull one pendulum back a short distance and let it go. As it swings back and forth, notice that the other pendulum also begins to move, picking up speed and amplitude with each swing. Notice that the pendulum you originally moved slows down with each swing and eventually stops, leaving the second pendulum briefly swinging by itself. But then the process begins to reverse, and soon the first pendulum is swinging again while the second one is stopped. The pendulums repeatedly transfer the motion back and forth between them this way as long as they continue to swing. Experiment with different wire lengths and with different string tensions to produce more strongly or weakly interdependent coupled pendulums.

What's Going On?

Every pendulum has a *natural* or *resonant frequency*, which is the number of times the pendulum swings back and forth per second. The resonant frequency depends on the pendulum's length. Longer pendulums have lower frequencies.

Every time the first pendulum swings, it pulls on the connecting string and gives the second pendulum a small tug. Since the two pendulums have the same length, the pulls of the first pendulum on the second occur exactly at the natural frequency of the second pendulum, so the second pendulum begins to swing too. The second pendulum swings slightly out of phase with the first one. That is, when the first pendulum is at the height of its swing, the second pendulum is still somewhere in the middle of its swing. As soon as the second pendulum starts to swing, it starts pulling back on the first pendulum. These pulls are timed so that the first pendulum slows down. To picture this, it may help you to think of a playground swing. When you push on the swing at just the right moments, it goes higher and higher. When you push the swing at just the wrong moments, it slows down and stops.

The second pendulum pulls on the first pendulum at just the "wrong" moments. Eventually, the first pendulum is brought to rest; it has transferred all of its energy to the second pendulum. But now the original situation is exactly reversed, and the first pendulum is in a position to begin stealing energy back from the second. And so it goes, the energy repeatedly switching back and forth until friction and air resistance finally steal all of it away from both pendulums.

If the two pendulums are not the same length, then the tugs from the first pendulum's swings will not occur at the natural frequency of the second one. The two pendulums swing but with an uneven, jerky motion.

○ ○ ○ ○ ○ ○ ○ **etc.** ○ ○ ○ ○ ○ ○ ○

It is easy to predict how often the two swinging cans will trade energy. Count the total number of swings per minute when you start both pendulums together and they swing back and forth, side by side. Compare that to the number of swings per minute when you start them opposite one another—that is, with one pulled forward and one pulled backward an equal distance from the string, and then released at the same time. The difference between those two numbers exactly equals the number of times per minute that the pendulums pass the energy back and forth if you start just one pendulum while the other hangs at rest. Physicists call these two particular motions *normal modes* of the two pendulum system, and they call the difference between the frequencies of the normal modes a *beat frequency*.

Descartes' Diver

To paraphrase the French philosopher René Descartes: "I sink, therefore I am."

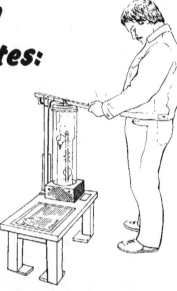

▶ Squeezing the sides of a plastic soda bottle changes the fluid pressure inside. Changes in fluid pressure affect the buoyancy of a Cartesian diver made from an eyedropper or a Bic™ pen. The diver floats, sinks, or hovers in response to pressure changes. There are two different versions to choose from here.

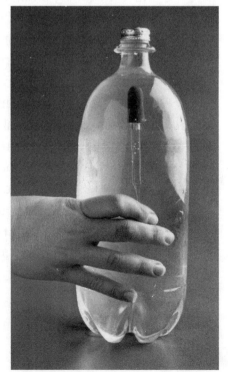

Materials

Eyedropper Diver

> ► An eyedropper.
>
> ► A tall drinking glass.
>
> ► Room-temperature water.
>
> ► One 2-liter soda bottle with screw-on cap.
>
> ► Optional: Thin, flat bottle (an empty dishwashing liquid or shampoo bottle, for instance).

Bic™ Pen Diver

> ► A Bic™ ballpoint pen with transparent plastic body.
>
> ► Pliers.
>
> ► A small lump of modeling clay the size of a pea.
>
> ► A tall drinking glass or wide-mouthed container.
>
> ► One 2-liter soda bottle with screw-on cap.
>
> ► Room-temperature water.
>
> ► Optional: Thin, flat bottle (an empty dishwashing liquid or shampoo bottle, for instance).

Assembly

Eyedropper Diver
(5 minutes or less)

Fill the tall drinking glass with room-temperature water. Gradually draw water into the eyedropper until the eyedropper floats in the glass with its top barely above the surface.

Fill the soda bottle almost to the top with room-temperature water. Transfer the eyedropper into the soda bottle. Be careful not to change the amount of water in the dropper while doing this. Screw the cap onto the bottle tightly.

Bic™ Pen Diver
(15 minutes or less)

Remove the ink cartridge from the pen with a pair of pliers: It will come out easily. Notice that the empty pen body is open at one end and plugged at the other. Attach a small amount of clay around the outside of the tube near the open end, without plugging the hole. This is just for weight.

You can use another bit of clay to plug the small air hole in the side of the tube, or you can leave the air hole unplugged, allowing the water to rise higher in the tube. If you like, you can also saw the tube off to a shorter length to make a smaller diver. If you shorten the tube or leave the hole open, you will need less clay to adjust the diver's buoyancy.

Test and adjust the diver by placing it open-end-down in the drinking glass or other wide-mouthed container. Add or remove clay until the diver floats with about ¼ inch (6.25 mm) sticking out of the water.

Fill the soda bottle almost to the top with room-temperature water. Place the diver open-end-down in the almost-full bottle, and screw the cap on tightly.

To Do and Notice
(5 minutes or more)

Squeeze the soda bottle to make the diver sink, rise, or hover at any depth. You also want to test your diver's responses in a thin, flat bottle, such as a bottle that originally contained dishwashing liquid or shampoo.

To add a little spice, you can decorate the top of the eyedropper so that it becomes a diver with a funny face, or find small, hollow, open-bottomed toy figures to use as divers. You can also decorate the bottle. Use your imagination and creativity!

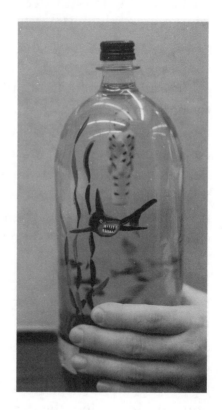

What's Going On?

The Greek philosopher Archimedes was the first person to notice that the upward force that water exerts on an object, whether floating or submerged, is equal to the weight of the volume of water that the object displaces. That is, the buoyant force is equal to the weight of the displaced water.

As you squeeze the bottle, you increase the pressure everywhere in the bottle. The higher pressure forces more water into the eyedropper, compressing the air in the eyedropper. This causes the dropper to displace less water, thus decreasing its buoyancy and causing it to sink. When you release the sides of the bottle, the pressure decreases, and the air inside the bulb expands once again. The dropper's buoyancy increases, and the diver rises. If you look carefully, you can see the level of water changing in the dropper as you vary the pressure on the bottle.

If you use a thin, flat bottle, squeezing on the wide sides of the bottle will increase the pressure inside the bottle, but squeezing on the narrow sides will cause the volume of the bottle to expand and the pressure inside to decrease. If you use such a bottle, adjust the weight or water content of a Cartesian diver so that it barely floats. When this diver reaches the bottom of the bottle, it will stay there, even when you stop squeezing on the wide sides. You must squeeze the narrow sides to drive the diver to the surface. It will then stay at the surface even when the squeezing stops.

The key to this behavior is to carefully adjust the diver initially, so that it barely floats. As the diver sinks, the pressure outside the diver increases slightly with the water's depth. This increase is in addition to the increase in pressure you cause by squeezing the bottle. When the diver reaches the bottom and you stop squeezing, the pressure resulting from the increase in depth remains and continues to compress the air bubble a little. If the diver has been carefully balanced, this small compression of the bubble will be enough to keep the diver submerged. The process reverses when you squeeze the narrow sides to raise the diver.

○ ○ ○ ○ ○ ○   **etc.**   ○ ○ ○ ○ ○ ○

Since ships float, their weight must be equal to the buoyant force of the water. The weight of a ship is therefore called its *displacement*.

Downhill Race

Two cylinders that look the same may roll down a hill at different rates.

▶ Two objects with the same shape and the same mass may behave differently when they roll down a hill. How quickly an object accelerates depends partly on how its mass is distributed. A cylinder with a heavy hub accelerates more quickly than a cylinder with a heavy rim.

Materials ▸ 2 identical round metal cookie tins (such as those from butter cookies).

▸ 10 large metal washers (about ¼ pound [112 g] each).

▸ Double-sided foam stick-on tape (or adhesive-backed Velcro™).

▸ A ramp.

Assembly
(15 minutes or less)

Arrange five of the washers evenly around the outside rim of the bottom of one tin. Stack five washers in the middle of the bottom of the second tin. In both cases, secure the washers with tape or Velcro™.

To Do and Notice
(15 minutes or more)

Place both tins at the top of the ramp. Be sure the tops are on. Ask your friends to predict which tin will reach the bottom of the ramp first. Release the tins and let them roll down the ramp. The tin with the mass closer to the center will always reach the bottom first.

What's Going On?

At the top of the ramp, both tins have identical potential energy, since both have the same mass and are at the same height. At the bottom of the ramp, each tin will have part of its original potential energy appearing as *linear* (or *translational*) *kinetic energy* and the rest appearing as *rotational kinetic energy.* Though both tins have the same total mass, each has this mass distributed differently. It is harder to get the tin with its mass distributed along the rim rotating than it is to get the tin with its mass concentrated at the center rotating. The tin with its mass at the rim will use a greater part of its original potential energy just to get rolling than will the tin with its mass concentrated at the center. Therefore the tin with its mass at the rim has less energy available to appear as translational kinetic energy, resulting in a lower linear speed. The tin with its mass concentrated around the rim will lose the race to the bottom of the ramp, and the tin with its mass concentrated at the center will win.

○ ○ ○ ○ ○ ○   **etc.**   ○ ○ ○ ○ ○ ○

The use of lightweight "mag" wheels on cars is related to translational and rotational kinetic energy. Imagine that you had two cars of equal overall mass, but one had lightweight "mag" wheels and a heavy chassis, and the other had heavy steel wheels and a light chassis. Given the same energy input, the "mag" wheel car would accelerate more rapidly, since less of the energy supplied would be needed to get the wheels rotating, and more would therefore appear as straight-line motion of the car as a whole.

It is interesting to experiment with rolling cans of soup down an inclined plane. Solid soups roll down the incline at a slower rate than liquid soups. The liquid does not have to rotate with the can, so the potential energy of the liquid soup can go into linear motion, not into rotation of the soup.

Drawing Board

A pendulum moving in two directions creates beautiful designs.

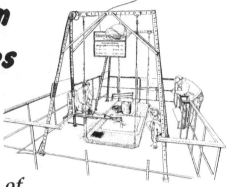

▶ The Drawing Board consists of
a marking pen that remains
stationary and a platform that
swings beneath the pen, acting as a pendulum. As
the platform swings, the pen marks a sheet of
paper that is fastened to the platform, generating
beautiful repetitive patterns, which grow smaller
with each repetition. These colorful designs contain
hidden lessons in physics.

Materials ▶ The easiest way to proceed is to use com-
mercially available toys such as Ellipto™
($22.00 from the Exploratorium Store) or
Pendul-Art™ (from toy stores). You can
also devise your own homemade versions
after looking at these products, or try to
build the large-scale version described on
page 48.

Make Your Own Version

▶ A ruler.

▶ One 4 × 4 × 12 inch (10 × 10 × 30 cm)
wood post.

▶ A nonskid base.

▶ A drill.

▶ A pivot bolt.

▶ 2 metersticks or yardsticks.

▶ Washers.

▶ Wire.

▶ Rubber bands.

▶ 3 large tables or 4 evenly spaced hooks in a
ceiling.

▶ A large board.

▶ 4 large hook eyes.

▶ Rope.

▶ Duct tape.

▶ Bricks.

▶ A large sheet of plain paper.

▶ Masking tape.

- ▶ Marking pens.
- ▶ Optional: String.
- ▶ Adult help.

Assembly
(5 minutes or less)

Set up the Ellipto™ or Pendul-Art™ according to the manufacturer's instructions. If you want to build your own Drawing Board, see the information on the next page.

To Do and Notice
(15 minutes or more)

Once the Drawing Board is adjusted, you can create wonderfully intricate designs. Try drawing one to four patterns on the same paper using pens of different colors, changing the direction and force of the push with each new color.

What's Going On?

When the platform is displaced from its rest position, the four suspending strings exert forces on it to bring it back. You can think of these forces as acting in two directions perpendicular to each other: "north-south" and "east-west," for example. The combination of these two simultaneous motions can produce a variety of curved forms, in the same way that proper simultaneous manipulation of the two knobs on an Etch-a-Sketch™ toy allows you to draw curves.

The diminishing size of each successive repetition of the pattern is a graphic demonstration of how friction steadily dissipates the energy of a moving object.

Make Your Own Drawing Board
(1 hour or less)

One of our teachers put together a large-scale version of the Drawing Board that was dramatic. Rather than attempting to give detailed instructions for assembling this device, we have chosen instead to supply some labeled drawings (see next page) and helpful hints. The rest is left to the dedicated experimenter.

- The penholder must be counterbalanced so that the pen exerts minimum pressure on the moving board while maintaining constant contact with the writing surface.
- You will have to adjust the length of the suspension ropes, since they stretch with time. Try using a knot called a *slip hitch*, shown on the next page.
- The placement of the weight on the board is critical. Experiment with various positions.
- One person pushes the board to start rotational as well as translational motion. Another person controls the penholder, lowering the pen to start drawing and raising it to stop.
- The Drawing Board should produce a pattern that repeats the same basic shape over and over again, with each cycle getting smaller. If the pattern is not consistent from one cycle to the next, try moving the weight on the board or adjusting the counterbalance weight on the penholder. Also make sure that the penholder is not shifting on the floor.

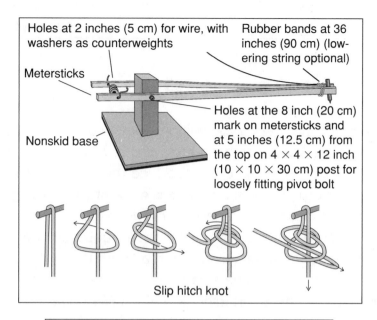

Holes at 2 inches (5 cm) for wire, with washers as counterweights

Rubber bands at 36 inches (90 cm) (lowering string optional)

Metersticks

Holes at the 8 inch (20 cm) mark on metersticks and at 5 inches (12.5 cm) from the top on 4 × 4 × 12 inch (10 × 10 × 30 cm) post for loosely fitting pivot bolt

Nonskid base

Slip hitch knot

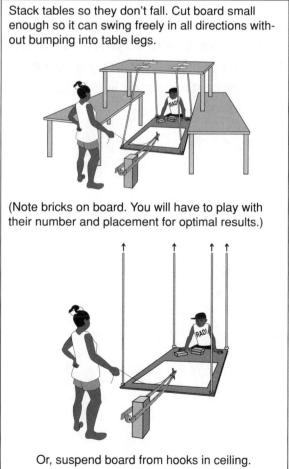

Stack tables so they don't fall. Cut board small enough so it can swing freely in all directions without bumping into table legs.

(Note bricks on board. You will have to play with their number and placement for optimal results.)

Or, suspend board from hooks in ceiling.

○ ○ ○ ○ ○ ○   **etc.**   ○ ○ ○ ○ ○ ○ ○

Some of the shapes you will produce with the Drawing Board are known as *harmonograms* or *Lissajous figures*. An oscilloscope can easily produce these figures, since the pattern on the scope face is generated by a single electron beam simultaneously moving vertically and horizontally on the screen. An oscilloscope can be thought of as an electronic Etch-a-Sketch™.

One of our teachers had this Snack set up and running during an aftershock of the 1989 Loma Prieta earthquake. The pen traced the pattern of motion generated by the aftershock. The operating principle behind the Drawing Board—a pen directly attached to the earth with a paper only loosely attached to the earth—is the operating principle behind a seismograph.

Falling Feather

Prove to yourself that Galileo was right!

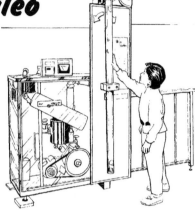

▶ In a famous demonstration, Galileo supposedly dropped a heavy weight and a light weight from the top of the Leaning Tower of Pisa to show that both weights fall at the same acceleration. Actually, this rule is true only if there is no air resistance. This demonstration lets you repeat Galileo's experiment in a vacuum.

Materials ▸ A clear, plastic, rigid-walled tube with at least a 1 inch (2.5 cm) inner diameter and at least 3 feet (90 cm) long. Available at your local plastic store. (Longer tubes show the effect more clearly.)

▸ A solid rubber stopper and a one-hole rubber stopper to fit in the ends of the plastic tube.

▸ A section of copper tubing about 4 inches (10 cm) long that fits tightly in the hole in the rubber stopper (glass tubing can be used if care is taken).

▸ A thick-walled flexible plastic or rubber vacuum tubing about 6 feet (180 cm) long.

▸ A coin and a feather (or a small piece of paper).

▸ A vacuum pump (use a regular lab vacuum pump if available; if not, use a small hand pump such as Mityvac®).

▸ 2 hose clamps.

▸ Adult help.

Assembly
(30 minutes or less)

Insert the solid stopper firmly into one end of the plastic tube. Put the coin and feather in the tube. Push the copper tube through the one-hole stopper, and firmly insert the stopper in the other end of the plastic tube. Push the vacuum tubing over the

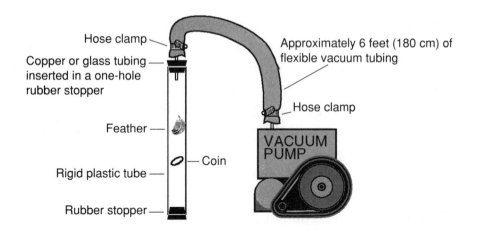

copper tube and secure it with a hose clamp, if needed. Attach the other end of the vacuum tubing to the pump; again, use a hose clamp if needed.

To Do and Notice
(15 minutes or more)

Invert the tube and let the objects fall. Notice that the feather falls much more slowly than the coin. Now pump the air out of the tube and invert it again (the pump can remain attached while you invert the tube). Notice that the feather falls much more rapidly than before—in fact, it falls almost as fast as the coin. Let the air back into the tube and repeat the experiment. (Try to avoid rubbing the wall of the tube; otherwise, static electricity may make the feather stick to it.)

What's Going On?

Galileo predicted that heavy objects and light ones would fall at the same rate. The reason for this is simple. Suppose the coin has

50 times as much mass as the feather. This means that the earth pulls 50 times as hard on the coin as it does on the feather. You might think this would cause the coin to fall faster. But because of the coin's greater mass, it's also much harder to accelerate the coin than the feather—50 times harder, in fact! The two effects exactly cancel out, and the two objects therefore fall with the same acceleration.

This rule holds true only if gravity is the only force acting on the two objects. If the objects fall in air, then air resistance must also be taken into account. Larger objects experience more air resistance. Also, the faster an object is falling, the more air resistance it feels. When the retarding force of the air just balances the downward pull of gravity, the object will no longer gain speed; it will have reached what is called its *terminal velocity*. Since the feather is so much lighter than the coin, the air resistance on it very quickly builds up to equal the pull of gravity. After that, the feather gains no more speed, but just drifts slowly downward. The heavier coin, meanwhile, must fall much longer before it gathers enough speed so that air resistance will balance the gravitational force on it. The coin quickly pulls away from the feather.

○ ○ ○ ○ ○ ○   **etc.**   ○ ○ ○ ○ ○ ○

The terminal velocity of a falling human being with arms and legs outstretched is about 120 miles per hour (192 km per hour)—slower than a lead balloon, but a good deal faster than a feather!

Momentum Machine

How ice skaters, divers, and gymnasts get themselves spinning and twisting faster.

► You've probably seen an ice skater spinning on the tip of one skate suddenly start to spin dramatically faster. A diver or gymnast may also suddenly flip or twist much faster. This speeded-up rotation results from a sudden redistribution of mass. You can make yourself suddenly spin faster while sitting in a rotating chair.

Materials ▶ A rotating stool or chair from a scientific supply house, an office supply store, or a classroom.

▶ 2 heavy masses. (2 bricks will do, but steel is even better.) Use the heaviest weights that you can support at arm's length.

▶ A partner.

▶ Adult help.

Assembly

No assembly is required.

To Do and Notice
(5 minutes or more)

Sit in a chair with one of the masses in each hand and with arms outstretched. Have your partner start rotating you slowly, then have that person let go and move away. Quickly pull the masses inward and notice that you rotate faster. Be careful! A very rapid spin may cause the chair to tip over! Also, you may be dizzy when you get up.

What's Going On?

Newton found that an object in motion tended to remain in motion, in a straight line and at a constant speed, unless it was acted upon by a net force. Today, we call this observation the *law of conservation of momentum*. The *momentum* of an object is the product of its mass and its velocity.

There is an equivalent law for rotating objects. A rotating object tends to remain rotating with a constant angular momentum unless it is acted upon by an outside twisting force. The definition of angular momentum is slightly more complex than that of linear momentum. *Angular momentum* is the product of two quantities known as *angular velocity* and *moment of inertia*. Angular velocity is merely velocity measured in degrees, or radians-per-second, rather than meters-per-second.

Moment of inertia depends on both the mass of an object and on how that mass is distributed. The farther from the axis of rotation the mass is located, the larger the moment of inertia. So your moment of inertia is smaller when your arms are held at your sides and larger when your arms are extended straight out.

If the motion of a rotating system is not affected by an outside twisting force, then angular momentum is conserved for this system, which means that the angular momentum stays the same.

A person sitting on a rotating chair or stool approximates a system in which angular momentum is conserved. The friction of the bearings on the chair stem serves as an outside twisting force, but this force is usually fairly low for such chairs. Since angular momentum is conserved, the product of angular velocity and moment of inertia must remain constant. This means that if one of these factors is increased, the other must decrease, and vice versa. If you're initially rotating with your arms outstretched, then when you draw your arms inward, your moment of inertia decreases. This means that your angular velocity must increase, and you spin faster.

○ ○ ○ ○ ○ ○   **etc.**   ○ ○ ○ ○ ○ ○

The conservation of angular momentum explains why an ice skater starts to spin faster when he suddenly draws his arms inward, or why a diver or gymnast who decreases her moment of inertia by going into the "tuck" position starts to flip or twist at a faster rate.

Nonround Rollers

A flat panel rolls smoothly on noncircular rollers, providing a decidedly counterintuitive experience.

▶ The most common closed and curved plane figure that has constant width as it rotates is the circle. Surprisingly, however, there are other figures that have this property. They have a variety of shapes that you can construct with a compass and straightedge. The rollers you can build with this Snack behave in seemingly paradoxical ways.

Materials ▸ Access to a photocopier.

▸ Scissors.

▸ Manila file folders, posterboard, or similar stiff material.

▸ A metric ruler.

▸ A drawing compass.

▸ Glue, tape, or stapler and staples.

▸ A piece of posterboard or masonite, about 6 × 18 inches (15 × 45 cm).

Assembly

In this Snack, we offer several options. You can use a predrawn template to build a simple nonround roller (Version 1), perform the geometric constructions for the rollers yourself (Version 2), or construct simple nonround rollers of your own design (Version 3).

Version 1:
Predrawn Template for the Simplest Nonround Roller
(30 minutes or less)

Photocopy the patterns in Figure 1 on the next page. Glue the entire photocopied sheet to stiffer material (manila folder or posterboard). Cut out the patterns. The large pattern is the axle, and the two smaller ones are the ends.

Fold the axle on the long horizontal lines to make a triangular prism. Fold Tab A over area A, and glue or tape them together.

Fold the axle flanges x and y outward. Staple or glue the axle flanges to the corresponding lettered areas on the ends.

Make a set of two (or three) such rollers.

Figure 1
Pattern for simple nonround roller

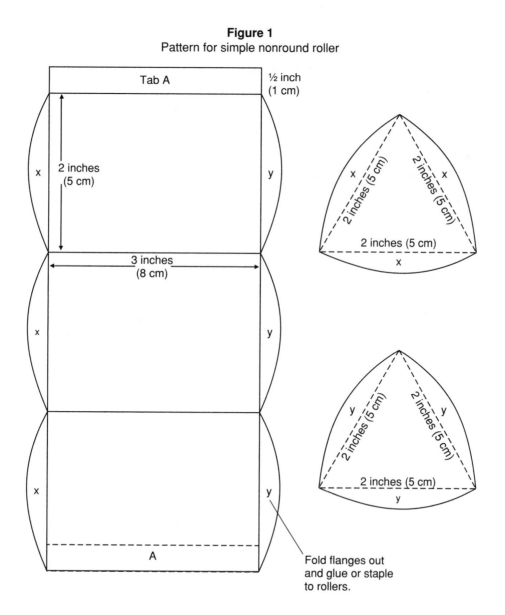

Version 2:
Geometric Constructions for the
Simplest Nonround Roller
(1 hour or less)

Follow Steps 1–4 in Figure 2 to construct an equilateral triangle with circular arcs connecting its vertices. We suggest you start with a triangle that is about 2 inches (5 cm) on a side. After you are familiar with the process, you can make larger versions. The name of this constant-width, nonround roller is the *Reuleaux triangle.*

On a piece of manila folder, draw four identical Reuleaux triangles. Cut them out. These will serve as the wheels for a set of two rollers.

Figure 2

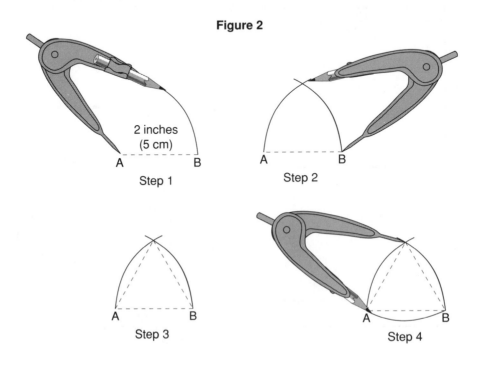

To make an axle, draw a rectangle measuring 3 inches × 6 inches (8 cm × 15 cm). Divide this into three smaller rectangles, each measuring 3 inches × 2 inches (8 cm × 5 cm). On one end, add a ½ × 3 inch (1 cm × 8 cm) tab. Finally, use the compass to make three arcs of radius 2 inches (5 cm) along each side of the three rectangles. Your drawing should be identical to the drawing in Figure 1.

Draw and cut out two axles for a set of two rollers. Assemble as noted in Version 1.

Version 3:
Geometric Construction of a General Case of Nonround Rollers
(1 hour or less)

Nonround, constant-width rollers of many different shapes can be made as noted in Steps 1–7 below and Figure 3 (next page).

Step 1: Draw a triangle of any size on a piece of cardboard. It does not have to be any particular type of triangle—any variety will do. Extend each side of the triangle beyond the triangle's vertices.

Step 2: Find the longest side of the triangle and open the compass so that its gap is a little longer than that side. (In the picture shown, the longest side is BC.) Set the compass at point B and make arc EF between BA and BC.

Step 3: Set the compass at point A, matching the pencil to point E. Make arc DE.

Step 4: Set the compass at point C, matching the pencil to point F. Make arc FG.

Figure 3

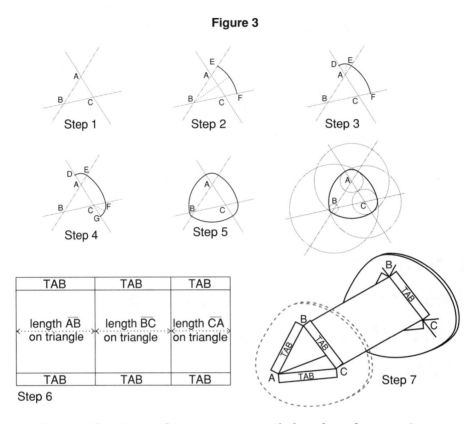

Step 5: Continue this process until the closed curve is complete.

If, after the first arc is made, one of the subsequent arcs ends up going into the triangle, then you will not be able to continue around the outside. If this happens, you should consider how the triangle might be redrawn to avoid this, and try again.

The drawing after Step 5 shows all the circles that contribute to the roller.

Step 6: Construct the axle by drawing a diagram similar to the one shown onto a piece of cardboard.

Step 7: Attach the axle to the roller ends. It is important that the roller ends be aligned with each other. The easiest way to accomplish this is to match the sides of the axle with the corresponding sides of the triangle.

To Do and Notice
(5 minutes or more)

Build at least two identical rollers. Put them on a flat surface. Place the piece of masonite or posterboard on top of the rollers and roll it gently from side to side. The rollers should roll smoothly and the board should stay level. (See the photo on page 59.)

There is no standard definition of the center of a nonround roller. Define your own center, and see if it stays a constant height above the surface on which the rollers are rotating. Notice that there is no point on the roller that stays a constant height as the roller rolls. Any point you choose will bob up and down.

What's Going On?

Versions 1 and 2

The roller always pivots on a vertex, even at the top and bottom, and the distance to the opposite contact point is always the same.

Version 3

The width of the nonround roller at any point is defined by a straight line that runs through one of the vertices of the triangle and through the triangle itself. Each such straight line is the sum of two radii—the radius of one large arc and the radius of one small arc. For example, the straight line PO in Figure 4 (next page) is the sum of the radii of arc HG (a large arc) and arc DE (a small arc).

Suppose you have a roller like the one shown in Figure 4. Let's say the roller is resting on point O. As the roller rolls on arc

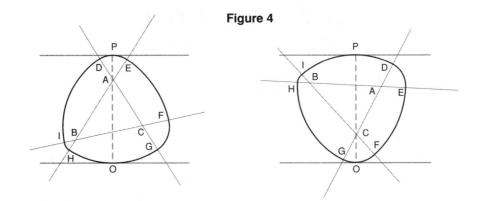

Figure 4

HG, with its resting point approaching H, the board on top of the roller will be rolling on arc DE. The board will remain level because the roller's width (which is the sum of the radius of arc DE and the radius of arc HG) will be constant.

Suppose the roller rolls until it rests on point H. Its width is still the sum of two radii—the radius of arc HI and the radius of arc EF. Since arc HI and arc HG have point H in common, and since arc DE and arc EF have point E in common, the width of the roller must still be constant. As the roller continues rolling and reaches point I, the same argument applies, and the width of the roller is always the same.

The rolling roller is shown in Figure 5 below.

When you tried to choose a center for your nonround roller, you might logically have chosen the triangle's centroid. Another logical choice would be the point halfway between the top and

Figure 5

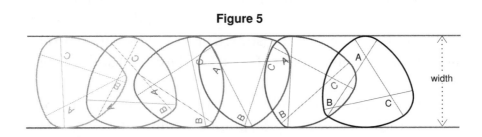

bottom of the roller for a particular orientation. Neither of these points, however, stays at a constant height as the roller rolls. Instead, they describe an up-and-down motion. As you observed, there is no point on the roller that stays a constant height as the roller rolls. For this reason, the rollers would make lousy car wheels. (Where would you put the axle?)

○ ○ ○ ○ ○ ○ **etc.** ○ ○ ○ ○ ○ ○

A drill bit made in the shape of a Reuleaux triangle can be used to drill a square hole! See the Mathematical Games section in *Scientific American*, February 1963, pp. 148–156.

Resonant Pendulum

Big swings from little pulls grow.

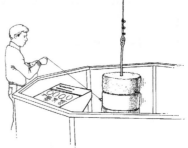

▶ By exerting very small forces at
just the right times, you can make
a massive pendulum swing back
and forth in very large swings.

Materials ► A metal paint can (1 gallon [3.8 *l*] size with lid). A sand-filled steel bucket will work, but the sand may spill.

► About 10 feet (3 m) of metal chain or strong rope.

► A large hook or eye bolt to attach the chain or rope securely to the ceiling.

► Sand to fill the paint can.

► A ceramic magnet on a few feet of string.

► Optional: A second magnet on a string.

► Adult help.

Assembly
(15 minutes or less)

Fill the paint can with sand, close the lid to prevent spills, and suspend it from the ceiling with the chain or rope. The can should hang somewhere between waist height and ground level. The closer to the ground it hangs, the less traumatic the results if it should somehow fall.

To Do and Notice
(15 minutes or more)

Stand a few feet away and throw the magnet at the can. Your goal is to get the magnet to stick to the can. Once you have done this, pull gently on the string to set the can in motion. If you pull too hard and the magnet pulls off, try again. By pulling very gently on the string, but only pulling when the pendulum is moving toward you, you can gradually make the pendulum swing in very large swings.

By using the second magnet on a string, a second person standing 90 degrees to the side of you can make the pendulum move along a diagonal line between the two of you by pulling gently at the same time that you do. If they pull out of phase with you, they can make the pendulum move in a circle.

What's Going On?

A very small force, when applied repeatedly at just the right time, can induce a very large motion. This process is known as *resonance.* Perhaps the most familiar example of resonance in everyday life is swinging on a playground swing. The first push or pump sets the swing in motion. Each subsequent push or pump is delivered at just the right time to increase the amplitude of swing. If you continue pushing or pumping over a period of time, the swing will gradually go higher and higher.

Every pendulum, from a playground swing to your hanging paint can, has a *frequency* at which it tends to swing. This is the pendulum's *natural frequency.* To find the natural frequency of a pendulum, just pull it to the side and release it. The pendulum will swing back and forth at its natural frequency. If the frequency of pushes on a pendulum is close to the pendulum's natural frequency, the motion and the pushes will remain in step. Each successive push will increase the amplitude of the motion of the object.

You can measure your pendulum's natural frequency using a stopwatch or a timer. Time how long it takes the pendulum to swing back and forth 10 times. Then divide this time by 10. You now have the *period* of one swing of the pendulum. The frequency is the inverse of the period. To get the frequency, just divide one by the period. For example, if 10 swings take 20 seconds, then the period is 2 seconds. The frequency is 1 divided by 2 seconds, or one-half of a cycle per second (one-half hertz, or ½ Hz).

○ ○ ○ ○ ○ ○ **etc.** ○ ○ ○ ○ ○ ○

This device can double as a dramatic potential-to-kinetic-to-potential energy demonstration. Pull the can to one side until it just reaches your nose. (Adjust the length of the rope as necessary to allow this.) Let go of the can (without pushing!) and stand very still (without moving your head forward!), and the pendulum will return repeatedly without striking your face. A bowling ball with a large eyebolt screwed into a predrilled hole can be substituted for the paint can in this demonstration, since no magnet is used and, hence, a metal can is not necessary. The paint can or bowling ball will not hit you in the nose, because of the *law of conservation of energy.* To swing farther, the pendulum must rise higher; to rise higher, it needs more energy. If no energy is added during the swing, the pendulum cannot hit you in the nose.

Resonant Rings

One reason not all buildings are equal in an earthquake.

► This device graphically demonstrates that objects of different sizes and stiffnesses tend to vibrate at different frequencies.

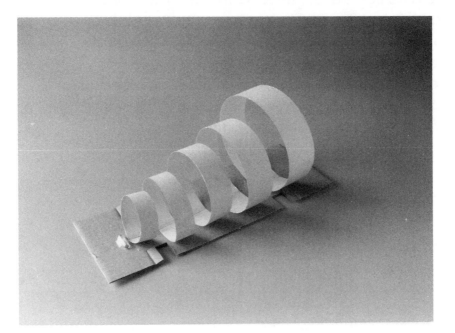

Materials ► A sheet of cardboard measuring 1 foot (30 cm) long and several inches wide.

► A large sheet of construction paper (about 14 × 20 inches [35 × 50 cm]).

► Masking tape or transparent tape.

Assembly
(15 minutes or less)

Cut four or five 1 inch (2.5 cm) wide strips from the construction paper. The longest strip should be about 20 inches (50 cm) long, and each successive strip should be about 3 inches (8 cm) shorter than the previous one. Form the strips into rings by taping the two ends of each strip together. Then tape the rings to the cardboard sheet as shown in the picture on the previous page.

To Do and Notice
(5 minutes or more)

Shake the cardboard sheet back and forth. Start at very low frequencies and slowly increase the frequency of your shaking.

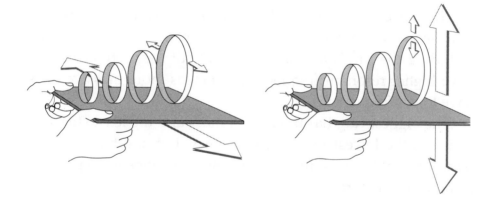

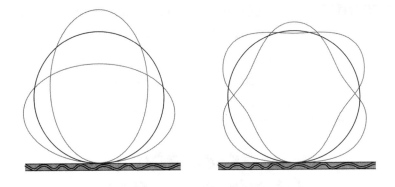

Notice that different rings vibrate strongly, or *resonate*, at different frequencies. The largest ring will begin to vibrate strongly first, followed by the second largest, and so on. The smallest ring starts to vibrate at the highest frequencies.

Keep shaking the cardboard faster and faster, and notice that the largest ring will begin to vibrate strongly again. Each ring will vibrate at more than one frequency, but the shape of each ring will be different for each resonant frequency.

The rings will also have different resonant frequencies if you shake the board up and down instead of sideways.

What's Going On?

The frequencies at which each ring vibrates most easily (its *resonant frequencies*) most easily are determined by several factors, including the ring's *inertia* (mass) and stiffness. Stiffer objects have higher resonant frequencies, whereas more massive ones have lower frequencies.

The biggest ring has the largest mass and the least stiffness, so it has the lowest resonant frequency. Put another way, the largest ring takes less time than the smaller rings to respond to an accelerating force.

During earthquakes, two buildings of different sizes may respond very differently to the earth's vibrations, depending on how well each building's resonant frequencies match the "forcing" frequencies of the earthquake. Of course, a building's stiffness—which is determined by the manner of construction and the materials used—is just as important as a building's size.

○ ○ ○ ○ ○ ○ **etc.** ○ ○ ○ ○ ○ ○

You can make the vibration frequency audible and more obvious by cutting a 1 inch (2.5 cm) section of plastic drinking straw, inserting a BB into it, taping paper over the ends of the straw, and taping the straw to the cardboard sheet parallel to the end. As you shake the sheet, the BB will tap against the ends of the straw at the same frequency as your vibration.

Resonator

If you vibrate something at just the right frequency, you can get a big reaction.

► *In this Snack, wooden dowels of varying lengths, each loaded with the same mass, are vibrated at identical frequencies. When the vibration matches the* **resonant frequency** *of one of the dowels, that dowel vibrates with a large amplitude. If you vibrate an object near one of its* **natural frequencies,** *its motion may grow to quite large values, a process known as* **resonance.** *Spectacular examples of resonance include the collapse of the Tacoma Narrows Bridge in a windstorm and the destruction of buildings during earthquakes.*

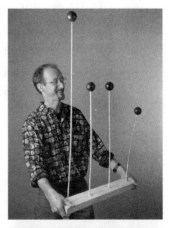

Materials ► Three ¼ inch (6 mm) wooden dowels measuring 1½ feet (45 cm) long, 2 feet (60 cm) long, and 2½ feet (75 cm) long.

► One ⅜ inch (9.5 mm) dowel measuring 2 feet (60 cm) long.

► 4 Superballs (or, if you can't find Superballs, you can substitute tennis balls or lumps of clay).

► One 2 × 4 (5 cm × 10 cm) measuring approximately 2 feet (60 cm) long.

► A drill.

► Optional: Carpenter's glue.

► Adult help.

Assembly
(30 minutes or less)

Drill four holes approximately 4 inches (10 cm) apart along the center line of the wide face of the 2 × 4 (5 cm × 10 cm). The first three holes should be slightly smaller than ¼ inch (6 mm), and the fourth hole should be slightly smaller than ⅜ inches (9.5 mm). Gently hammer the dowels into the holes so that they are held firmly in place. (If you prefer, you can drill holes that are the same size as the dowels and glue the dowels into the holes with carpenter's glue.)

Drill a ¼ inch (6 mm) hole halfway through three of the Superballs and a ⅜ inch (9.5 mm) hole halfway through the fourth Superball. The best way to do this is to place the balls in a good vise and to drill slowly.

Place a Superball on the end of each dowel. The Superball adds a relatively large mass to each dowel.

The experiment will work even if you don't put Superballs on the dowels, but the balls lower the resonant frequencies and make the motion easier to see. You can also substitute tennis balls or lumps of clay for the Superballs. Since the center of a tennis ball is hollow, however, the ball tends to flop around on the end of the dowel.

To Do and Notice
(15 minutes or more)

Grip the 2 × 4 inch board at each end and slide it back and forth across a tabletop, moving it lengthwise. As you vary the rate of shaking, different dowels will swing back and forth with greater or lesser amplitude. When you are shaking at just the right frequency to cause one dowel to vibrate violently, another dowel may hardly be vibrating at all.

Notice which dowels vibrate violently at lower frequencies and which vibrate violently at higher frequencies. (CAUTION: If you get the dowels vibrating too violently—watch out!—they may break!)

What's Going On?

When you push a person on a swing, a series of small pushes makes the person swing through a large amplitude. To accomplish this, you time your pushes to match the swing's natural frequency, the rate at which the swing tends to move back and forth.

The same principle is at work in this Snack. When you shake the 2 × 4 assembly at just the right frequency, a series of small shakes adds up to a large vibration of a particular dowel. The shaking board sets the dowel vibrating. If the next shake is timed just right to reinforce the next vibration of the dowel, the vibration in the dowel builds up. This process of using a series of small inputs to create a large motion is known as *resonance.*

The longer the dowel, the more slowly it tends to vibrate—the lower its natural frequency. Thus, the long dowel will resonate at lower frequencies than the short dowel.

Stiffer dowels have higher resonant frequencies. The ⅜ inch (9.5 mm) dowel is much stiffer than the ¼ inch (6 mm) dowels, and so it tends to resonate at higher frequencies than the thinner dowels.

Each dowel may have more than one resonant frequency.

○ ○ ○ ○ ○ ○ **etc.** ○ ○ ○ ○ ○ ○

Just as each dowel has its natural frequencies of vibration where resonance occurs, so most objects tend to vibrate at certain frequencies. You may have noticed that parts of your car rattle at a certain speed or that certain objects vibrate and buzz in response to a particular note from your stereo. These are everyday examples of resonance.

Resonance has also been responsible for some spectacular destruction. In earthquakes, buildings are often damaged when the frequency at which the ground is shaking comes very close to or matches one of the resonant frequencies of the buildings. The Tacoma Narrows Bridge vibrated itself to pieces when a strong wind pushed it at just the right frequency. The wing of the Lockheed Electra jet failed repeatedly until engineers discovered that the wing's resonant frequency was responsible for its destruction. A suspended walkway at a Kansas City hotel collapsed when people dancing on the structure caused resonant vibration.

In the army, troops always march across a bridge out of step; army vehicles are spaced at irregular intervals when crossing a bridge. These practices avoid setting up vibrations at the bridge's resonant frequency.

Not all objects resonate. Any object that dissipates energy faster than the energy is added will not resonate. Try, for example, shaking the dowels under water. The friction of the dowel moving through water will dissipate the energy faster than you add it. Since the motion of the dowel will not build up at any frequency, there is no resonance.

Soap Bubbles

Create geometric art with soap films.

▶ *Using pipe cleaners and drinking straws, you can make three-dimensional geometric frames: cubes, tetrahedrons, or shapes of your own design. When you dip these frames in a soap solution, the soap films that form on the frames are fascinating and colorful.*

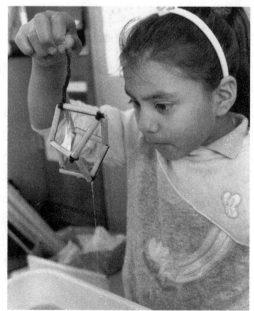

Materials ▸ Plastic drinking straws.

▸ Pipe cleaners (available at school supply, hobby, or party stores).

▸ A small bucket or container for the bubble solution. The container must be large enough so that bubble frames are entirely covered when they are dipped.

▸ Bubble solution (You can use a commercial solution like Wonder Bubbles™, or use the Exploratorium's recipe: To each gallon (3.8 *l*) of water add ⅔ cup (160 ml) of Dawn™ or other dishwashing liquid and 1 tablespoon (15 ml) of glycerine, available at your local pharmacy. Bubble solution works best if it is aged at least a day before use.)

Assembly
(30 minutes or less)

Form frames using the drinking straws for the straight pieces. Connect two straws at a corner by inserting a doubled pipe cleaner into the end of each straw. In places where three straws meet, fold the pipe cleaners as shown in the diagram on the next page. Attach a pipe cleaner handle to your frame.

Try constructing cubes or tetrahedrons, or just let your imagination run wild. Mix the soap solution in the bucket. Make sure that you have enough solution to fully cover the frames when they are dipped.

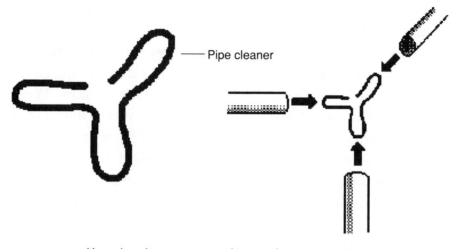

How pipe cleaners are used to attach straws together.

To Do and Notice
(15 minutes or more)

Dip the frames into the soap solution, and observe the fascinating geometrical shapes that the soap films form. Also notice the shimmering colors in the soap film.

What's Going On?

As you lift your frame out of the solution, the soap film flows into a state of *minimum energy*. The soap film is in a state of minimum energy when it's covering the least possible amount of surface area. The intricate shapes you see inside the frame represent the minimum area the soap film can cover. You may notice that a soap film will sometimes take on different shapes when you dip the frame into the solution again and again. That's because there may be more than one way for the soap film to form a minimum surface area.

When light waves hit the soap film, they reflect and interfere with each other. This interference causes the shimmering colors you see. White light is made of many different colors. When white light shines on the soap film, some light waves reflect from the front surface of the film and some reflect from the back surface of the film. When these two sets of reflected waves meet, they can add together, cancel each other out, or partially cancel, depending on the thickness of the film and the initial color of the light. When light waves of a particular color meet and cancel each other, then that color is subtracted from white light. For example, if the red light waves cancel, then you see white light minus red light, which you perceive as blue-green light.

○ ○ ○ ○ ○ ○   **etc.**   ○ ○ ○ ○ ○ ○

Plastic bar straws, which have a smaller diameter than regular drinking straws, hold the pipe cleaners more tightly. But bar straws are more expensive and are sometimes harder to get. If you can't find them at grocery or liquor stores, try restaurant or party supply stores.

Spinning Blackboard

Create graceful loops and spirals by drawing on a spinning disk.

► When you draw on a spinning disk, you make unexpected patterns. You may draw a straight line, for instance, but what appears on the disk is a spiral. The patterns you make result from adding the motion of your hand to the spinning motion of the disk.

Materials ► An old record player or turntable. (A lazy Susan with a square or circular board placed on it will also work, but it has to be rotated by hand.)

► Paper and marking pens or butcher paper and sand.

► Optional: A cardboard disk.

Assembly
(15 minutes or less)

For the marking pen version, simply mount a piece of paper on the turntable. (If the turntable has grooves in it, cover it first with a sheet of cardboard.)

For the sand version, fit a large piece of butcher paper between the turntable and the body of the record player to protect the mechanism from the sand. Cover the turntable with a cardboard disk. Spread a thin layer of sand evenly on the cardboard disk and start the turntable. (CAUTION: Use only a junk turntable if you use this method, because sand and precision turntables don't mix.)

To Do and Notice
(15 minutes or more)

Start the turntable rotating. Move a marking pen at a constant speed in a straight line from the center of the turntable to the edge. (On the sand-covered turntable, trace the straight line with your finger.) Notice the spiraling curve that appears on the turntable. This curve is called a *spiral of Archimedes*. Move your pen or finger out from the center at different speeds and notice how the spiral changes.

Try drawing other straight lines: For example, start at the edge of the turntable and draw a line toward the center, or start at the edge and draw a line making a 45-degree angle with the edge. Draw straight lines with different constant speeds to make new curves.

Draw many straight lines radiating out from a point halfway between the center and the edge of the turntable. Try to draw a triangle or a square on the rotating turntable.

What's Going On?

When you draw a straight line from the center of the spinning turntable toward a point on the wall of the room, the turntable rotates beneath your finger as you draw the line. Your finger traces a curve on the turntable. Since record players rotate clockwise, the line appears to curve to the left, when viewed from its starting point, which was at the center.

The spiral made by your finger also appears to curve to the left. The pattern on the turntable shows the motion of your finger from the perspective, or *frame of reference*, of a speck of sand on the spinning turntable. (Physicists would say that the speck of sand is in a *rotating frame of reference*.)

Objects move in a straight line at a constant speed when there are no net forces on them. The person drawing the straight line can see no net forces on the pen or fingertip, but a person rotating with the turntable sees the pen or fingertip curve in an arc and so believes that there must be a force pushing it into this curved path. In the rotating frame of reference, observers make up forces named *centrifugal* and *Coriolis* to explain the curvature of the line.

○ ○ ○ ○ ○ ○   **etc.**   ○ ○ ○ ○ ○ ○

Like a speck of sand on the turntable, a person on the
surface of the earth is in a rotating frame of reference.
You can picture the earth as a giant turntable. If you
are in the southern hemisphere looking north toward
the equator, the earth is rotating clockwise. If a jetliner
or a wind or an ocean current were traveling in a
straight line from the south pole toward the equator,
you'd see them curve to the left.

From the northern hemisphere, the earth appears
to rotate counterclockwise. Objects moving from the
north pole toward the equator appear to curve to the
right of their direction of motion. In fact, objects
moving in any direction appear to curve to the right.
This explains why air flowing into the low-pressure
center of a hurricane in the northern hemisphere
bends to the right, and so flows around the hurricane
in a counterclockwise direction.

Strange Attractor

The attraction and repulsion of magnets produces entrancing, unpredictable motion.

▶ *Patterns of order can be found in apparently disordered systems. This pendulum—a magnet swinging over a small number of fixed magnets— is a very simple system that shows chaotic motion for some starting positions of the pendulum. The search for order in the chaos can be very engrossing.*

Materials ► A ring stand and a clamp.

► 4 to 6 ceramic magnets (available at Radio Shack).

► Paint, masking tape, or correction fluid.

► Fishing line or string.

Assembly
(15 minutes or less)

Put all the magnets together in a stack so that they stick together magnetically. By doing this, you are orienting the magnets so that all of the north poles point in one direction and all of the south poles point in the other direction. Mark the top of each magnet with paint, tape, or correction fluid, thus identifying all the matching poles.

Use the string or fishing line to hang one magnet from the ring stand so that it is a free-swinging pendulum. You can hang the magnet in any orientation.

Arrange the other magnets on the ring stand base in an equilateral triangle measuring a couple of inches on a side. Position the magnets so that they all have the same pole up.

Adjust the length of the pendulum so that the free-swinging magnet will come as close as possible to the magnets on the ring stand base without hitting them or the base itself. You can accomplish this either by changing the length of the string or by adjusting the position of the clamp.

To Do and Notice
(15 minutes or more)

Give the pendulum magnet a push, and watch!

Vary the location and poles of the magnets to develop other patterns. You can arrange the magnets so that all of them have the same pole up, or you can mix them up. Notice that a tiny change in the location of one of the fixed magnets or in the starting position of the pendulum magnet may cause the pendulum to develop a whole new pattern of swinging.

What's Going On?

The force of gravity and the simple pushes and pulls of the magnets act together to influence the swinging pendulum in very complex ways. It can be very difficult to predict where the pendulum is going to go next, even though you know which magnets are attracting it and which are repelling it.

This sort of unpredictable motion is often called *chaotic motion*. Strangely enough, there can be a subtle and complex kind of order to chaos. Scientists try to describe this order with models called *strange attractors*.

○ ○ ○ ○ ○ ○ **etc.** ○ ○ ○ ○ ○ ○

The new sciences of chaos and turbulence are unveiling hidden relationships in nature. Diverse phenomena, such as the patterns of Saturn's rings, measles outbreaks, and the onset of heart attacks all follow chaotic patterns.

Often, a system that is predictable in the long run shows chaotic variations in the short run. Although it is quite difficult to predict specific daily weather behavior in the San Francisco Bay Area, the overall long-term patterns are generally known. The individual motion of insects may be random and insignificant, yet the behavior of the population as a whole can be analyzed.

As shown in this Snack, a very slight difference in the starting position of the pendulum can grow to a tremendous difference in the pattern of motion in a short time. This is characteristic of chaotic systems. Weather scientists recognize this characteristic of chaos when they argue over the "butterfly phenomenon." That is, can a butterfly flapping its wings in China drastically alter the weather in New York?

For further reading, see: *Chaos* by James Gleick (Viking Penguin, 1988) and *The Turbulent Mirror* by John Briggs and F. David Peat (HarperCollins, 1990).

Take It from the Top

How does this stack up?

▶ Simple wooden blocks can be stacked so that the top block extends completely past the end of the bottom block, seemingly in a dramatic defiance of gravity. To make this work, you must start moving the top block first and then proceed on down the stack, rather than starting from the bottom up. A mathematical pattern can be noted in the stacking.

Materials ▶ Approximately 15 to 20 uniform, flat, and rectangular blocks. (The particular size is not crucial, as long as all blocks are the same. We have found that 1 × 4 × 9 inch [2.5 × 10 × 22.5 cm] finished pine works well.)

Assembly

See "To Do and Notice."

To Do and Notice
(15 minutes or more)

Stack the blocks evenly on top of one another to make a vertical column. Position the stack so that you are facing the long side of the blocks. Start at the top of the stack. Move the top block to the right so it overhangs the second block as far as possible without falling. Now move the top two blocks to the right as a unit so they overhang the third block as far as possible without falling. Move the top three blocks, and continue on down the stack. How many blocks must you move before the top block is completely beyond the balance point?

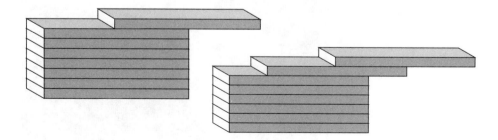

Notice that you can never move a given block over as far as you moved the previous one. The larger the stack of blocks you are moving, the smaller the distance you can move them before they become unbalanced and topple over.

What's Going On?

When you move the top block over so that it just balances, its *center of gravity,* or balance point, rests over the edge of the block below. Each time you move a block over, you are finding the center of gravity of a new stack of blocks—the block you move plus the blocks above it. The edge of each block acts as a fulcrum supporting all the blocks above it.

By considering the positions of the centers of gravity of the blocks as the stack is built, it can be shown that the first block will be moved ½ of a block length along the second block, the top two blocks will be moved ¼ of a block length along the third block, the top three blocks will be moved ⅙ of a block length along the fourth block, the top four blocks will be moved ⅛ of a block length along the fifth block, and so on. Do you see the pattern?

How far will the *n*th block be moved along the block below it? The answer is: $\frac{1}{2}n$ of a block length along the $n + 1$ block. Unavoidable experimental error due to factors such as nonuniformity of blocks and inexact location of balance points will lead to actual values that are not quite in agreement with theory but that are still probably close enough to make the point.

○ ○ ○ ○ ○ ○   **etc.**   ○ ○ ○ ○ ○ ○

Textbooks provide an instantly available set of uniform "blocks." Teachers might try stacking the books as we have described when passing them out to students.

Other readily available stackable objects include flat rulers, index cards, or playing cards. You can also cut pieces of matte board or masonite to any desired size; this method is particularly handy if you want to make lots of smaller sets for individual use.

If you want to have some fun, glue together a duplicate set of the blocks that you stacked earlier. You can do this quickly with hot glue. Place the glued stack on top of a loose block that has a strong string attached to a screw eye in one end. You now have a great inertia demonstration. If you jerk the bottom block out swiftly, you won't upset the stack. Practice this a few times first, though! Also, be careful that the block you jerk doesn't hit someone! You will likely have more success if you position the bottom block with the screw eye facing away from the overhanging portion, rather than below it. You might also consider fudging a little by not quite moving each block to its extreme balance point before gluing it. If you manage to jerk the bottom block out before your audience discovers that the stack is glued, they will think that this is an amazing feat. (A little creative showmanship and acting can set the stage for this!) You can also find the center of gravity of the glued stack, and show that the pivot point of the whole glued stack is directly under the center of gravity.

Vortex

Whirling water creates a tornado in a bottle.

▶ *Water forms a spiraling, funnel-shaped vortex as it drains from a 2-liter soda bottle. A simple connector device allows the water to drain into a second bottle. The whole assembly can then be inverted and the process repeated.*

Materials ► Two 2-liter soda bottles.

► A Tornado Tube™ plastic connector (available from science museums, science stores, novelty stores, and some scientific supply companies). Or you can make your own using a washer with a ⅜ inch (9.5 mm) hole and electrical tape.

► Optional: A small dropper bottle of food coloring and/or bits of paper.

Assembly
(5 minutes or less with the Tornado Tube; 15 minutes or less with the washer and electrical tape)

Fill one of the soda bottles about two-thirds full of water. For effect, you can add a little food coloring or paper bits to the water. Screw the bottles onto both ends of the plastic connector. (CAUTION: Do not screw the connector on too tightly!) Or tape the bottles together with the washer between them.

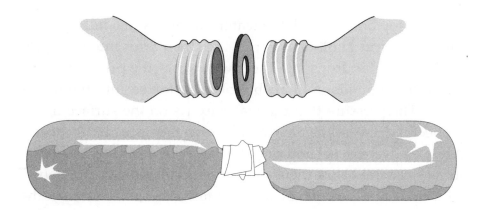

To Do and Notice
(15 minutes or more)

Place the two bottles on a table with the filled bottle on top. Watch the water slowly drip down into the lower bottle as air simultaneously bubbles up into the top bottle. The flow of water may come to a complete stop.

With the filled bottle on top, rapidly rotate the bottles in a circle a few times. Place the assembly on a table. Observe the formation of a funnel-shaped *vortex* as the bottle drains.

Notice the shape of the vortex. Also, notice the flow of the water as it empties into the lower bottle.

You can make the vortex with a single bottle by twirling the bottle and holding it over a water basin or the ground to drain, but you lose the water and have to refill the bottle each time you use it.

What's Going On?

When the water is not rotating, *surface tension* creates a skinlike layer of water across the small hole in the center of the connector.

If the top bottle is full, the water can push out a bulge in this surface to form a bulbous drop, which then drips into the lower bottle. As water drops into the lower bottle, the pressure in the lower bottle builds until air bubbles are forced into the upper bottle. The pressure that the water exerts on the surface in the connector decreases as the water level in the upper bottle drops. When the water level and pressure drop low enough, the water surface can hold back the water and stop the flow completely.

If you spin the bottles around a few times, the water in the upper bottle starts rotating. As the water drains into the lower bottle, a vortex forms. The water is pulled down and forced toward the drain hole in the center by gravity. If we ignore the small friction forces, the *angular momentum* of the water stays the same as it moves inward. This means that the speed of the water around the center increases as it approaches the center of the bottle. (This is the same reason that the speed of rotating ice skaters increases when they pull in their arms.)

To make water move in a circle, forces called *centripetal forces* must act on the water. These "center pulling" forces are provided by a combination of air pressure, water pressure, and gravity.

You can tell where the centripetal forces are greater by looking at the slope of the water. Where the water is steeper, such as at the bottom of the vortex, the centripetal force on the water is greater. Water moving with higher speeds and in smaller radius curves requires larger forces. The water at the bottom of the vortex is doing just this, and so the wall of the vortex is steepest at the bottom. (Think about race cars: Racetracks have steeper banks on high-speed, sharp corners to hold the cars in their circular paths around the track.)

The hole in the vortex allows air from the lower bottle to flow easily into the upper bottle. This enables the upper bottle to drain smoothly and completely.

○ ○ ○ ○ ○ ○ **etc.** ○ ○ ○ ○ ○ ○

Vortices occur in nature in many forms: Tornadoes, whirlpools, weather systems, galaxies, etc.

The essence of a vortex is that objects are drawn together toward the center, then miss!

Spiral waves form in the water surface of the vortex. These waves appear to move in slow motion as they travel upward through the downward flowing water.

The Exploratorium's *Vortex* exhibit was created by artist Douglas Hollis.

Water Spinner

Rotating water has a curved surface.

▶ When you spin a tank of water on a lazy Susan, the surface of the water forms a curve called a **parabola**.

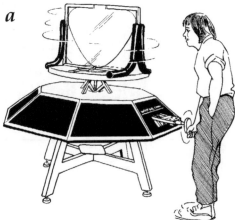

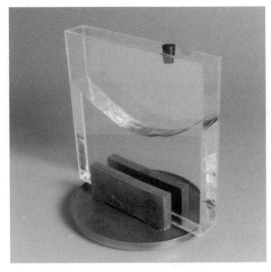

Materials ► A clear, thin, rectangular plastic box, about 12 × 12 × 1 inches (30 × 30 × 2.5 cm). (You can buy one ready-made, or you can easily glue one together from pieces of plastic available at a plastics store.)

► Silicone seal adhesive to make the box waterproof.

► A lazy Susan with a diameter bigger than the length of the box. (A Rubbermaid™ lazy Susan or another inexpensive household variety will work well.)

► 2 wood or plastic blocks, each about 2 × 6 × ½ inches (5 × 15 × 1.3 cm), to fasten the box to the lazy Susan.

► Tap water.

► Strong glue.

Assembly
(15 minutes or less with a ready-made box; one hour or less if you make your own box)

The seams of the box need to be watertight, so use the silicone seal adhesive to plug any leaks. Either cut a hole in the top of the box, or leave the top of the box open.

Glue the blocks to the lazy Susan alongside the box, to hold the box firmly in place.

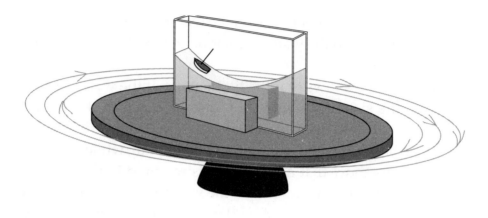

To Do and Notice

Half-fill the box with water and rotate the lazy Susan. Notice the shape of the surface of the water.

What's Going On?

When the waves on the rotating water surface settle down, the surface forms a curve called a *parabola*. As the box spins, the water tends to continue moving in a straight line tangent to the circle. However, the box restrains the water and forces it to keep moving in a circle. The water near the edge of the box goes around in one large circle in the same time that the water near the center goes around in a small circle. That means the water near the edge travels faster than the water near the center. The faster an object moves in a circle, the larger the force necessary to hold it in the circle. This force is called the *centripetal force*.

The surface of a body of water in equilibrium is always

perpendicular to the net forces on the water. The diagram below shows the forces on the water in relation to the tilt or slope of the water surface.

The diagram shows that the tilt or slope of the water surface indicates the size of the force holding the water in its circular path. The flat bottom of the parabola shows that little force is needed to hold the water there in its circular path, while the steep outer regions show that a large force is required in those areas.

You can prove to yourself that the water forms a parabola. A parabola has the equation $y = x^2$. Draw a parabola on a piece of graph paper and tape the paper to one side of your rectangular box so that you can look through the box and see the paper. Then rotate the box until you find the speed at which the bottom of the parabola you drew matches up with the lowest part of the water surface. The water surface should exactly match the curve of the parabola drawing at every other point.

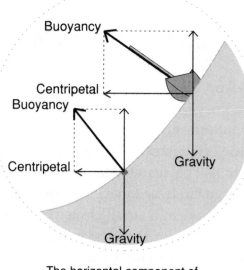

The horizontal component of the buoyancy provides the centripetal force.

○ ○ ○ ○ ○ ○ **etc.** ○ ○ ○ ○ ○ ○

Make a raft small enough to float inside your rotating box. A small, flat piece of wood with a toothpick mast works well. Place the raft on the water surface near the edge of the box, and then spin the box. The raft will stay in place even when it is on the slope of a hill of water. Its mast will always be perpendicular to the water.

Index

Page numbers in italics indicate illustrations relevant to the topic.